FAMILIES AROUND THE WORLD

A family from
ETHIOPIA

Julia Waterlow

RSVP
RAINTREE
STECK-VAUGHN
P U B L I S H E R S
The Steck-Vaughn Company

Austin, Texas

FAMILIES AROUND THE WORLD SERIES

A family from **BOSNIA**   A family from **GUATEMALA**

A family from **BRAZIL**   A family from **IRAQ**

A family from **CHINA**   A family from **JAPAN**

A family from **ETHIOPIA**   A family from **SOUTH AFRICA**

A family from **GERMANY**   A family from **VIETNAM**

Cover: The Getu family outside its home with all its possessions
Title page: The Getu family
Contents page: A trader at the local market

Picture Acknowledgments: The photographs in this book were taken
by Shawn G. Henry. The photographs were supplied by
Material World/Impact photos, and were first published
by Sierra Club Books, in 1994. © Copyright Shawn G. Henry/
Material World. The map artwork on page 4 is by Peter Bull.

© Copyright 1998, text, Steck-Vaughn Company

Published by Raintree Steck-Vaughn Publishers,
an imprint of Steck-Vaughn Company

Library of Congress Cataloging-in-Publication Data
Waterlow, Julia.
A family from Ethiopia / Julia Waterlow.
p. cm.—(Families around the world)
Includes bibliographical references and index.
Summary: Describes the activities of an extended family living near
the Ethiopian village of Moulo, providing brief information about
the country's daily life and customs.
ISBN 0-8172-4900-1
1. Family—Ethiopia—Juvenile literature.
2. Ethiopia—Social life and customs—Juvenile literature.
[1. Family life—Ethiopia. 2. Ethiopia.]
I. Title. II. Series: Families around the world.
HQ692.W37   1998
306.85'0963—dc21   97-499

Printed in Italy. Bound in the United States.
1 2 3 4 5 6 7 8 9 0 02 01 00 99 98

Contents

Introduction

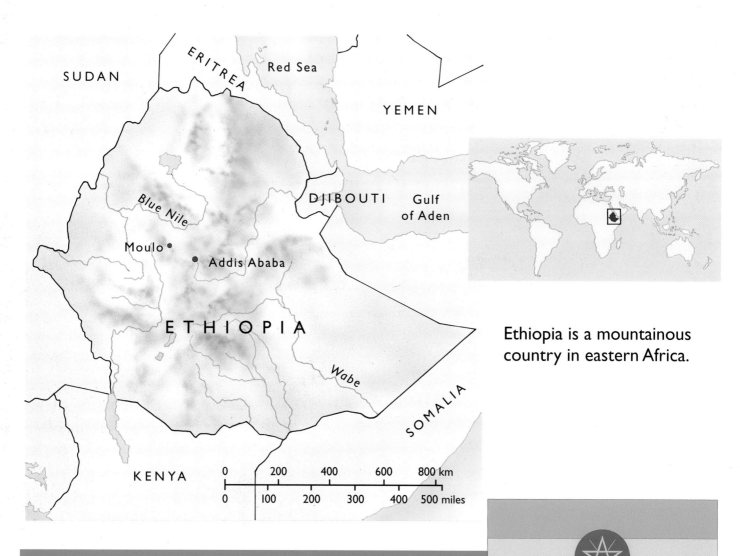

Ethiopia is a mountainous country in eastern Africa.

REPUBLIC OF ETHIOPIA

Capital city: Addis Ababa

Size: 437,494 sq. mi. (1,222,000 sq. km.)

Population: 55,900,000

Language: Amharic, Arabic, and about 75 local languages

People: Mainly Amhara or Oromo, many smaller groups

Religion: Orthodox Christian, Muslim, and African beliefs

Currency: Birr

THE GETU FAMILY

Size of household:	seven
Size of home:	322 sq. ft. (30 sq. m.)
Workweek:	Getu: 80 hours Zenebu:126 hours
Most valued possessions:	Oxen (Getu and Zenebu); Sheep (Teshome)
Family income:	$123 each year

The Getu family is an average Ethiopian family. The Getus have put everything they own outside their home so this photograph could be taken.

Meet the Getu Family

A TROUBLED COUNTRY

Ethiopia is a beautiful country in eastern Africa with mountains and hills. After war, famines, and terrible droughts there is now peace. Ethiopia is looking forward to a better future.

1 Getu, father, 30
2 Zenebu, mother, 25
3 Teshome, son, 10
4 Like, daughter, 8

5 Mamoosh, son, 7
6 Mulu, daughter, 3
7 Kebebe, son, 8 months

The Getu family lives together in a house with two rooms. Getu's mother, father, two sisters, and his brother and his family live next door. Fences around the houses keep in all the animals. Some of these are oxen, cattle, sheep, chickens, dogs and horses. The houses are surrounded by fields. Nearby is the village of Moulo.

"During the troubles we had to leave our home, but now we're back."—*Getu*

A House in Moulo

Many of the houses in Moulo have thatched roofs like this one. Getu's brother, Abera, who has more money, has a tin roof on his house.

FAMILIES STICK TOGETHER

Ethiopian families usually have several children. People often live in large family groups. Some people lost members of their families or their homes during the recent wars and droughts in Ethiopia. Even for people who did not, it is still very difficult to make ends meet.

◀ Zenebu cuddles the children asleep on the floor. Their cushion is made of cowhide.

A Welcoming Fire

The Getus have one room where they cook, eat, and sleep. They have a bed and some benches made from planks of wood. There is a small room on one side where the family stores its food.

In the evenings the family gathers around the fire and talks. The Getus' house does not have electricity. There is no running water in the house. Zenebu goes every day with the other women to collect water in clay jars from the well across the field.

▲ Inside the Getus' house a smoky fire is always burning.

9

Inside the House

Zenebu combs Mulu's hair. She always makes sure the family is clean and tidy.

With the help of the older children, Zenebu collects dung from the cows. She mixes it with straw and mud to make a paste. She then uses the paste to cover the walls of the house. To decorate the walls inside, Zenebu mixes some ash from the fire with water to make a white paste. She uses this like paint.

Because there are no windows, the family leaves the door open to let in the light. Sometimes the smaller animals go into the house. Zenebu doesn't mind about the chickens, but she always asks Teshome to keep the sheep out.

▼ Like is very proud of the painted decorations on the inside walls of the house.

"Mother makes patterns on the walls with a paste. There are even some handprints."—*Like*

Food and Cooking

The Getus don't use plates, knives, and forks. Instead, everyone eats with their hands. The food is served from one big dish.

A TASTY DISH

This is a typical Ethiopian meal. Underneath is *injera*, the soft, dark, spongy bread that Ethiopians make. On top of the dish is *wat*, a kind of spicy stew, and eggs.

Spicy Stew

The Getus like to eat *injera* bread with their meals. Zenebu cooks it in a big, wide pan. Sometimes the family has eggs with *wat*. On special occasions, they have meat or chicken.

Zenebu puts the food on a basket or tray and everyone helps themselves. Often other members of the family come and join the family for the evening meal. This is their main meal of the day. Zenubu always serves the men first and then eats her food afterward.

"I tear bits off my bread and dip them into the stew."—*Teshome*

13

Using a mortar and pestle, Zenebu pounds grain into flour for making bread.

Home-grown Food

The women grind the grain they grow in the fields to make flour for *injera* bread. Sometimes Zenebu roasts a special kind of grain to make *kolo,* which is a bit like popcorn. The Getus eat *kolo* for breakfast.

The Getus produce most of the food they eat themselves. As well as grain, they grow several different kinds of vegetables. The chickens provide eggs, and the cows give them milk and butter. But Zenebu still has to go to the market to buy some things such as coffee and salt.

Zenebu cooks *injera* bread on the fire in the house.

Working Hard

The oxen are the most valuable things the family owns.

FARMING

Most Ethiopians are farmers. They work hard and try to live off the food that they grow themselves. Many Ethiopians keep cattle. There are more cattle in Ethiopia than in any other country in Africa.

Out in the Fields

Getu is a farmer. He plows the fields and plants grain twice a year. Getu also has cattle that he and Teshome take out to graze. The family depends on its crops and animals for food. One of the most important times of year is when the rains come and the brown land turns green. If there is no rain, the fields have to be watered by hand with buckets brought from the well.

"When the crops grow well, all the hard work seems worthwhile."
—*Getu*

Women's Work

Zenebu and the other women help with planting
and watering in the fields. They also take care of
the house and family. The women must also
chop up firewood, bring water from the well, and
cook and wash.

Zenebu uses animal dung to make fuel for the fire. She mixes it with straw and makes it into big, round cakes. These burn well when they've been dried out in the sun. Since wood is not always easy to find, dung is very important to the Getus. Zenebu also uses dung to spread on the walls of the house.

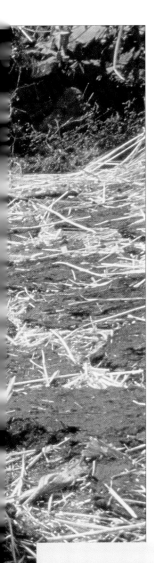

One of Zenebu's jobs is to chop wood for the fire.

"Most of my day is spent searching for dung!"— *Getu's sister-in-law, Ayeletch*

Making ends meet

The Getus have very little money and cannot afford to buy new clothes. Their clothes are second-hand ones from the market. If they need money, they have to sell one of their cows. Zenebu has started selling chicken eggs to make extra money.

Like's main job is to look after baby Kebebe, who spends much of the day strapped to Like's back.

The children help their parents as soon as they are old enough. The three older ones help Zenebu by carrying water and wood and feeding the animals. Teshome usually has to take the sheep out every day to graze. Like often keeps an eye on the small children.

"These are my sheep. It is my job to look after them."—*Teshome*

School and Play

EDUCATION

Only about 25 percent of children in Ethiopia go to school regularly. Children go to school for five hours a day, but all of the classes are in the morning. Few Ethiopian families can afford to send their children to school.

None of the Getu children go to school, although their cousin Zalalem does.

Only Getu can read and write. The Getu children have never been to school. Like Zenebu and her daughters, most women in Moulo have never been taught to read and write.

Getu plans to send Teshome to school next year but it will be difficult for the family to pay. The school is free, but the family will have to buy Teshome's books, paper, pens, and pencils. Teshome will also need a second set of clothes, one for school and one for working in the fields. The Getus' nearest school teaches in the local language, rather than Amharic, the main language in Ethiopia. Teshome would have to learn Amharic to find a good job and get ahead.

"I like to make up games with my cousin. We play with things we find around the house."
—*Mulu*

There are only about fifty students at the school nearest Moulo.

Spare Time

The rich coffee grown in Ethiopia is served whenever friends or family visit.

Some people in Ethiopia are Orthodox Christians. This is one of the oldest forms of Christianity in the world. Other people are Muslims.

Going to Church

The Getus are Orthodox Christians but are too busy to go to church every Sunday. They should not eat meat on Wednesdays and Fridays. This is not too difficult for the Getus because they don't often eat meat anyway!

"Our religion means we are not allowed to plow the fields or cut the grain on Saturday or Sunday."— *Local priest*

Coffee Time

Three times a day, the Getus' relatives gather together for coffee and to talk. Zenebu prepares and serves the coffee. She grinds the coffee beans and brews the coffee. Then she pours it out for the men. The women have their coffee after the men.

Zenebu and Ayeletch prepare coffee, pouring it into the special cups to serve the men and guests.

The Getus always welcome visitors, whether they are friends or strangers. Passersby are often asked in and invited to share the Getus' coffee, food, and firelight.

"The men always sit around, drinking coffee and chatting."
—*Zenebu*

"It takes three hours to walk to the big market."—*Zenebu*

The family rarely goes far beyond its house. Zenebu has to go once or twice a week to the market. The nearest one is about an hour away.

The Future

"I hope for peace everywhere so that all our problems will get better."—*Getu*

Getu has seen years of war in Ethiopia and wishes for peace all over the world. He hopes for money to buy better seeds and tools to help with the farming. Getu also wants more oxen and another horse. Zenebu would like to be able to buy the family some more clothes.

Most of all, Getu and Zenebu believe the children must go to school if they are to do well in the future. Getu would really like Teshome to become a pilot, but Teshome insists that he is going to be a farmer just like his father.

A teacher watches while three children take an exam at the school near Moulo. Teshome may be going to this school soon.

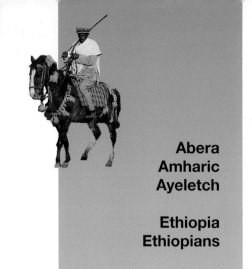

Pronunciation Guide

Abera	Ah-**bear**-ah
Amharic	Am-**har**-ick
Ayeletch	Eye-el-letch
Ethiopia	Ee-thee-oh-pee-ah
Ethiopians	Ee-thee-oh-pee-uns
Getu	Geh-two
injera	In-**jear**-ah
Kebebe	Keh-**beh**-beh

Like	Lee-kay
Mamoosh	Mah-moosh
Moulo	Moo-loh
Mulu	Moo-lou
Teshome	Teh-**show**-mee
Zalalem	Zah-**lah**-lem
Zenebu	Zeh-**neh**-boo

Glossary

Ceremony A special occasion when things are done in a particular way.

Civil war A war between people of the same country.

Compound An area that is surrounded by a fence.

Conquer To beat in a battle or war.

Drought A long time without rain.

Election A vote to choose new leaders.

Famine When there is very little food and people go hungry.

Grain The hard seed of plants, such as corn or wheat.

Independent Able to make your own decisions about how to act.

Mortar and pestle Grain is put in a hollowed-out chunk of wood (mortar) and pounded with a heavy piece of wood (pestle) to make flour.

Muslim Someone who follows the Islamic religion.

Orthodox Keeping strictly to tradition.

Oxen Another word for cattle, sometimes used to describe cattle that are used for plowing.

Well A hole dug to get water out of the ground.

Books to Read

Gilkes, Patrick. *Conflict in Somalia and Ethiopia*. Conflicts. Morristown, NJ: Silver Burdett Press, 1994.

Glaser, Elizabeth and Biel, Timothy L. *The Ethiopian Famine*. World Disasters. San Diego: Lucent Books, 1990.

Regan, Colm and Cremin, Pedar. *Africa*. Continents. Austin, TX: Raintree Steck-Vaughn, 1997.

Stewart, Gail B. *Ethiopia*. Places in the News. Morristown, NJ: Silver Burdett Press, 1991.

Index